Original title:
Crisp Echoes Beneath the Phoenix Bark

Copyright © 2025 Swan Charm
All rights reserved.

Author: Swan Charm
ISBN HARDBACK: 978-1-80559-336-2
ISBN PAPERBACK: 978-1-80559-835-0

The Pulse of Gaia's Resilience

In the heart of the forest's sigh,
Roots weave stories, old and spry.
Leaves whisper tales of ancient grace,
Nature's dance, a steady pace.

Mountains stand, their shadows cast,
Embers flicker, memories vast.
Rivers carve paths in stone,
Gaia's strength forever shown.

From ashes rise the vibrant green,
Life's tenacity, ever keen.
Through storms and trials, she will thrive,
In her embrace, we come alive.

Silhouettes Dancing in the Firelight

Beneath the stars, the flames ignite,
Shadows whisper, lost in the night.
Laughter rings, a joyous sound,
Feet take flight, no ties are bound.

The sparks ascend, a fleeting flight,
Carrying dreams into the night.
Around the glow, we spin and sway,
As time blends into warmth's embrace.

Flickering tales of love and fear,
In moments shared, we draw near.
Each heartbeat echoes in the dark,
Sealed forever, each glowing spark.

Nectar of Dreams from Scorched Soil

In the cracks where sorrow slept,
Longing seeds are gently kept.
From charred remains, new life will spring,
As nature dons her vibrant ring.

The sun descends, a silent grace,
Painting colors on life's face.
Petals unfurl from ash and stone,
Whispers of hope softly grown.

Sweet nectar flows from trials faced,
Nature mends, her scars embraced.
In weary hearts, the dreams ignite,
From scorched earth, we find our light.

Epiphany in the Wake of the Blaze

When flames have danced and light laid bare,
Wisdom rises from the air.
In silence, truths begin to form,
From chaos springs a brand-new norm.

Ashes speak of trials past,
Lessons learned, shadows cast.
With every breath, a chance to rise,
New resolve beneath the skies.

In the stillness, voices call,
Inviting courage, one and all.
Through the heart of loss, we gain,
An epiphany from the pain.

The Resounding Birthright of the Flame

In the heart it flickers bright,
An ember born from darkest night.
Crafted dreams ignite the air,
Awakening the silent flare.

With whispers soft, the shadows sway,
Guided by the light's ballet.
Through trials faced, the spirit grows,
Unyielding, as the fire flows.

Silent Echoes of the Reclaimed Earth

In twilight's hush, the past returns,
Amidst the soil, the candle burns.
From silent cries, a voice will rise,
Beneath the gaze of ancient skies.

Roots entwined in stories told,
Of quiet strength, and hearts so bold.
The echoes dance on breezes light,
Embracing dreams in the gentle night.

A Palette of Embered Memories

Brushstrokes of time on canvas spread,
With colors born from love and dread.
Each hue a tale, each shade a sigh,
Whispers of yesteryears drift by.

In flickering flames, the stories wake,
A vibrant world for memory's sake.
Tales of laughter, shadows cast,
Alive within the embers vast.

From Ashes to Sacred Whisper

From ashes low, the spirit climbs,
Transcending fears through space and time.
In softest tones, the truth reveals,
A tapestry of all it feels.

Sacred whispers call the day,
Guiding hearts along the way.
From molten warmth, new visions sprout,
In the eternal dance, no doubt.

The Language of Dance in the Blackened Leaves

In twilight's hush, the shadows sway,
The leaves respond, a soft ballet.
Whispers of wind, secrets unfold,
Beneath the boughs, stories retold.

Nature's rhythm, a pulse so clear,
Each rustling leaf holds tales to hear.
The forest floor, a stage embraced,
As dancers weave, their steps interlaced.

Beneath the stars, in moonlight's glow,
The language speaks where few would go.
With every twirl, a spirit freed,
In blackened leaves, they dance, they heed.

Rebirth in the Lina of Smoked Shadows

From ashes rise, a muted flame,
In shadows deep, no one to blame.
The echoes call, to life anew,
In Lina's heart, the world breaks through.

Each smoky breath, a tale of past,
In quiet strength, the die is cast.
Through fleeting dreams, the veils do part,
Rebirth begins within the heart.

A midnight sky, adorned with stars,
Transformation near, where healing scars.
Embrace the dusk, the dawn will show,
The dance of life, in colors flow.

When Silence Beckons Among the Ashes

Amidst the rubble, a stillness grows,
In quietude, the truth bestows.
Where fire once roared, now whispers dwell,
In ashes' touch, there lingers spell.

A moment pauses, breaths collide,
In woven silence, souls abide.
The night enfolds, a shroud of peace,
Amongst the ashes, heartbeats cease.

In shadows deep, the echoes blend,
When silence calls, we learn to mend.
From cinders cold, a warmth ignites,
Among the ashes, hope ignites.

Reverberations of Ancient Flames

In hollowed caves, the whispers hum,
Reverberations of the drum.
Ancient flames light paths once tread,
Where stories linger, ancestors led.

Each flicker speaks, a language bold,
Of battles fought, and tales retold.
In fiery glow, spirits align,
Ghosts of the past in shadows entwine.

Echoes reverberate, time suspended,
In fiery dance, all is defended.
From ashes rise the knowledge gained,
In ancient flames, the truth remains.

Sibilant Shadows of the Rebirth

In twilight's hush, they softly glide,
Echoes of dreams where spirits bide.
Whispers weave through the silent air,
Sibilant shadows, a dance so rare.

From ashes cold, a flicker starts,
Restoring hope to weary hearts.
In the cradle of night, they sing,
Of the joys that dawn will bring.

Beneath the stars, old tales revive,
Carried by winds, they feel alive.
With every sigh, the darkness fades,
In sacred circles, light invades.

The moonlight's grace, a gentle hand,
Brings forth new life, a radiant strand.
Through veils of mist, the truth shines bright,
Sibilant shadows embrace the light.

Vibrant Whispers of the Ashen Sky

Amidst the gray, a color blooms,
As whispers rise from muted tombs.
Voices carry on the breeze,
Vibrant echoes, the heart's unease.

Beneath the weight of ashen hue,
Hope flickers faint, yet still feels true.
In the silence, a song renews,
Painting skies with vibrant views.

Stars emerge like scattered seeds,
Planting dreams in twilight needs.
Each note lingers, soft and clear,
A call to all who choose to hear.

The world awakes from somber sleep,
In every crevice, secrets seep.
With every breath, the shadows break,
Vibrant whispers, the dawn will wake.

Resounding Cries from Embered Roots

From deep below, the echoes rise,
Resounding cries beneath the skies.
In ancient woods, the stories weave,
Of roots that grip, and hearts that grieve.

Through burning flames, the past returns,
Lessons learned as passion burns.
In every crack, a voice resounds,
Ember whispers in sacred grounds.

The dance of fire, so fierce and bright,
Paints the darkness with its light.
With every spark, a heartbeat found,
Resounding cries from the underground.

Memories clash like storms at sea,
Transforming pain to melody.
Each echo a promise, bold and true,
From embered roots, we start anew.

The Return of the Fiery Lament

In shadows cast by fading light,
A fiery lament ignites the night.
It stirs the soul with echoing pain,
Calling forth the lost refrain.

From ashes cold, the flames arise,
Burning bright in the velvety skies.
Each tear shed fuels the blaze,
Illuminating forgotten days.

Voices tremble in the storm,
As embers flicker, soft and warm.
With every heartbeat, we ascend,
The fiery lament, it will not end.

In the dusk, we find our voice,
From anguish deep, we make a choice.
To rise as one, to break the chains,
The return of hope, the fire reigns.

Sonnet of the Reborn Spirit

In shadows deep, a whisper stirs the night,
A flicker glows where once was only dark.
The heart beats slow, but surely finds the light,
Awakened now, the dormant spirit sparks.

From ashes rise the dreams that once were lost,
With every breath, the chains begin to break.
Embrace the storm, though voices may exhaust,
The soul now dances, finding joy awake.

In love's embrace, the past is set aside,
The journey blooms like flowers in the spring.
With every step, the old ways cast aside,
Reborn anew, the spirit starts to sing.

Beneath the Scorched Silhouette

The sky hangs low with burdens yet untold,
A canvas draped in shades of crimson fire.
Beneath the weight, the earth begins to mold,
New life emerges, driven by desire.

The shadows stretch, they whisper secrets old,
While fractured ground reveals a tale of pain.
Yet through the cracks, a beauty to behold,
Resilience blooms despite the harshest rain.

In weary hearts, a spark begins to glow,
Each breath of hope ignites the darkest night.
Beneath the scorch, the strength within must flow,
A rise from ruins brings the soul to flight.

The Murmurs of Renewal

In stillness rests the promise of the dawn,
The whispers call, a gentle lingering sound.
With each new turn, the past begins to yawn,
Awakening the peace that will surround.

The brook that flows sings tunes of sweet release,
A melody that wraps the heart in grace.
From every struggle comes a new-found peace,
In nature's rhythm, find your sacred space.

The leaves may fall, but roots remain so strong,
In every cycle, life finds ways to grow.
The murmurs call, inviting to belong,
To trust the journey, let the spirit flow.

Phoenix Trails through Silent Grove

In twilight's hue, the phoenix starts its flight,
With embered wings igniting boundless skies.
Through silent groves, it dances in the light,
A radiant path where shadows never rise.

The trees lean close, their branches intertwine,
To listen closely to the flames that soar.
They understand the heart's need to align,
With every breath, the spirit seeks for more.

Through whispered winds, the ancient tales unfold,
Of journeys paved with love and lingering dreams.
In every heart, the fire's warmth takes hold,
And thus the phoenix paints the world with gleams.

Where the Ashes Weep and Laugh

In the quiet dusk, shadows play,
Ashes whisper truths of yesterday.
They dance with sorrow, then rise with glee,
In their fragile bodies, a tale to see.

Laughter rings deep like a distant chime,
Weeping for moments that slip through time.
Each burnt remnant, a story told,
Of dreams engulfed in the fire's hold.

Yet here they bloom, in the ashen night,
Mirrored spirits that find the light.
From charred remains, new life will start,
In every ember flickers the heart.

Ashes may weep, but they also cheer,
For life's resilience, year after year.
In cycles of loss, there's beauty too,
Where laughter mingles with shadows anew.

Tapestry of Vibrance in the Burnt Hollow

In the hollowed land where embers glow,
Vibrant threads of nature's flow.
Colors emerge from grief's embrace,
A tapestry woven, a warm, soft grace.

Bright petals burst from scattered ash,
Nature renews in a brilliant flash.
Winds carry tales of life once sparked,
In every rustle, a promise marked.

From charred remains, wildflowers rise,
Gracing the earth beneath sunlit skies.
A dance of hues, both bold and bright,
In the heart of loss, the gain of light.

So let the burnt hollow's spirit sing,
Of nature's magic, and the joy it brings.
For every end births a start anew,
In this vibrant quilt, life finds its hue.

The Whispered Secrets of Nature's Fire

In flickering flames, secrets reside,
Nature breathes softly, a magical guide.
To listen closely to the night's sigh,
Is to hear stories that never die.

Each spark a whisper from earth to sky,
Carried by winds that rush and fly.
In the dance of fire, the truth is spun,
An ancient tale of all that's begun.

Through the smoke, visions appear,
Ghosts of the past hover near.
With every crackle, a name is called,
Echoes of moments that have not stalled.

So heed the flames, their comfort and fury,
They speak of existence, both wild and blurry.
In the heart of the fire lies nature's art,
A whispering secret, where all things part.

Lullabies of the Ashen Spirits

In twilight's embrace, the ashes sing,
Lullabies soft, of forgotten spring.
Whispers of dreams in shadows unfold,
Tales of the brave, the young and old.

As night descends, the spirits sway,
In the ashen cradle where they play.
Through sighing winds, their songs drift wide,
In the quiet, their beauty does abide.

Fragments of life weave through the dark,
Each note a memory, a flickering spark.
Burnt offerings lingering, sweet, and light,
Guiding the lost through the starry night.

So hush now, dear, let hearts be still,
Listen to secrets that dreams fulfill.
For in every ash, a spirit thrives,
In the lullaby's glow, the soul survives.

Harmony Among the Supernova Ashes

In the void where stars once shone,
Echoes of beauty, now overthrown.
Galaxies whisper their ancient lore,
Amongst the ashes, they sing once more.

Fragments glimmer in the dark,
Life anew from dust, a spark.
Silent cries of forgotten light,
In harmony, they greet the night.

Time transcends in cosmic dance,
Every heartbeat, a fleeting chance.
Within the remnants, hope does gleam,
In the ashes, we dream the dream.

Colors blend in the vast expanse,
Chaos sways to a radiant trance.
Among the ruins, creation thrives,
In the aftermath, the cosmos drives.

Together, we find our place,
In the remnants of a stellar grace.
With tender touch, we weave our fate,
Among supernovae, we resonate.

Where Shadows Bloom in Embers

In twilight's grasp, the shadows weave,
Flickering lights, we hardly believe.
Amidst the dark, blooms brightly grow,
Faint shimmering traces, a gentle glow.

Embers dance on the whispering breeze,
Secrets linger beneath the trees.
Softly they speak of a bygone flame,
In shadows, we're never quite the same.

The night holds secrets, stories untold,
Where warmth lingered, the bitter grows cold.
Yet, from the ashes, hope can arise,
In glowing embers, the heart defies.

Each flicker tells of battles fought,
In the quiet night, dreams are sought.
Where the unseen dares to roam,
In shadows, we find a hidden home.

With open hearts, we face the dark,
Accepting the fear, igniting the spark.
For where shadows bloom, love shall embark,
In the embers, we find our mark.

Songs of the Eclipsed Dawn

When night swallows the sun's bright cheer,
In eclipsed beauty, we draw near.
The world pauses in breath and sigh,
As shadows stretch beneath the sky.

Whispers cradle the sleeping light,
Enchanting dreams in the velvet night.
Silhouettes dance in the soft refrain,
A haunting lull of joy and pain.

Wings of night, on silence glide,
Carrying secrets where dreams abide.
In the stillness, our hearts collide,
As stars wink out, we swallow pride.

From the darkness, a new day will rise,
Hope unfurling in brighter skies.
The dawn will break through every fight,
In its embrace, we find our light.

We sing our songs of times gone by,
Where shadows linger and hopes can fly.
For in the eclipse, we learn to see,
The beauty in moments, wild and free.

Whispers of the Afterglow

In the stillness when night descends,
The afterglow gently extends.
Hearts whisper secrets of what's passed,
In lingering warmth, memories cast.

Fading light paints the world anew,
Soft touches of pink and gold hue.
Shadows stretch as the day departs,
In the twilight, we open our hearts.

Night unveils tales of long-lost dreams,
In soft murmurs, the universe gleams.
Stars awaken, blink above our heads,
In the quiet, the unsaid spreads.

With each breath, the silence hums,
A symphony of the night that comes.
In afterglow, we find our way,
Guided by longing, night turns to day.

Fleeting moments, forever retained,
In whispers, the essence of love is gained.
For in the afterglow's soft embrace,
We hold the night in a tender space.

Serenades of the Rejuvenated Grove

In the heart of the green so bright,
Whispers call to the soft moonlight,
Leaves dance gently in the warm breeze,
Life awakes with the rustling trees.

Songs of old fill the fragrant air,
Nature's chorus beyond compare,
Roots entwined in a lover's embrace,
Every corner, a sacred place.

Birds find nests in cradles high,
Baby blooms stretch to the sky,
Squirrels prance with tales to share,
Joy abounds everywhere.

Sunlight filters through the shade,
Casting dreams that never fade,
In this grove, the soul can mend,
A haven where hearts transcend.

Nightfall brings stars wrapped in dew,
Ancient secrets, whispered anew,
Embrace the night, let worries cease,
In the grove, we find our peace.

Melodies in the Wake of the Fire

Embers crackle, stories ignite,
Whispers drifting into the night,
Flames dance wonders, shadows play,
Time pauses, the world fades away.

In the glow, dreams find their way,
Carried in the smoke, they sway,
Summer's warmth holds hearts so near,
Every moment, crystal clear.

Soft laughter rings, a tune sublime,
Melodies woven, transcending time,
Voices harmonize 'neath the stars,
A chorus born from wounds and scars.

The fire's song wraps around our hearts,
Binding souls as the night departs,
Through the flames, we learn to live,
In every spark, we learn to give.

As dawn approaches with gentle grace,
Leaving behind the night's embrace,
Memories linger, sweet and bright,
Melodies born in the wake of light.

Shadows that Dance in Tomorrow's Glow

In the twilight, shadows align,
Silhouettes whisper tales divine,
Moments brushed by the golden hue,
Time stands still, for me and you.

Beneath the stars, dreams take their flight,
Lost in the magic of the night,
Each flicker sparks our hearts to race,
In this quiet, we find our place.

Tomorrow's glow calls us to rise,
With hope that twinkles in our eyes,
Embrace the dawn, let shadows chase,
Stepping into the light's embrace.

Hearts entwined with the rising sun,
In every shadow, we find the fun,
Fear dissolves with the night's retreat,
In tomorrow's warmth, we feel complete.

As we journey through night and day,
Our shadows dance in bright array,
Together we soar, hearts aglow,
In tomorrow's embrace, we bravely grow.

Echoes of Resilience in the Twilight

As the sun bows to the evening star,
Echoes linger, near and far,
Whispers of strength in gentle sway,
Resilience blooms at the end of day.

Through trials faced, we learn and strive,
With every heartbeat, we come alive,
Stars glimmer where darkness reigned,
Hope, like fire, remains unchained.

In twilight's glow, courage unfolds,
A tapestry woven with stories bold,
Each thread a tale of love and pain,
In unity, we break every chain.

The world spins on, yet we remain,
Unyielding hearts, bound by the same,
Together we rise, against the tide,
In echoes of love, forever abide.

As night blankets the earth in grace,
We find our strength in every space,
In the twilight, we mend and grow,
Resilience shines, our spirits aglow.

Firelight Poetry on Nature's Canvas

The flames dance bright in the night,
Whispers of warmth in the dark's embrace.
Colors flicker, shadows take flight,
Nature's art in a glowing space.

The forest breathes a tale untold,
Leaves rustle gently, a murmured sigh.
Golden embers, red, and bold,
Light the path where memories lie.

In every crackle, stories unfold,
Of creatures unseen, of owls that call.
A canvas alive, painted in gold,
Where firelight dances, and shadows fall.

Glimmers of magic in every spark,
Illuminating the depths of the wood.
Painting whispers on a canvas dark,
In nature's embrace, the hearts understood.

So gather around, find solace here,
In the fire's glow, let your spirit flow.
For in this moment, the world feels near,
Firelight poetry, where wild hearts grow.

Ashen Enigmas of the Woodland

In the hush of dusk, shadows stir,
Beneath the branches, secrets lie.
Whispers of leaves, a gentle blur,
In the heart of the woods, where echoes sigh.

Ashen remnants mark the ground,
Ghosts of flames that once did blaze.
Tangled roots in silence bound,
Reveal the past through the smoky haze.

Mossy stones hold tales of old,
Echoes of life in every crevice.
Stories of fire, fierce and bold,
Now just shadows, a tranquil service.

The melody of the night fulfills,
With every breeze, the woods awake.
In ashen layers, nature thrills,
A tapestry woven, the earth's heart aches.

So wander deep, past the dying light,
Seek the enigmas wrapped in the trees.
In the woodland's embrace, find your flight,
Among ashen whispers, seek the keys.

Beneath the Charred Echoes of Time

Beneath the ashes, whispers reside,
Memories linger, like smoke in air.
Time dances softly, with every tide,
In charred remains, secrets to share.

The bark tells tales of what has been,
Of moments lost to fiery rage.
Life's resilience found within,
In the scars of earth, a vibrant page.

Old trees stand guard, stoic and proud,
Witnesses to the change they have faced.
A silent vow, beneath the shroud,
That nature rebuilds, never erased.

Among the remnants, new blooms spring,
A testament to the cycle of life.
Beauty emerges from everything,
In the heart of darkness, free from strife.

So listen closely, hear the ground,
Echoes of time whisper in peace.
Beneath the charred, life will be found,
In the quiet strength, the soul's release.

Soulful Murmurs from the Scorched Earth

In the silence of earth, tales arise,
From ashes deep, a story unfolds.
Murmurs of nature, beneath the skies,
Speak of struggle and beauty behold.

The sunlight warms the scorched terrain,
Healing touch to the land's warm heart.
From charred remains, life will regain,
A soulful journey, a vivid start.

With every breeze, the spirits sway,
A dance of hope in the air so sweet.
The land remembers, come what may,
In every heartbeat, life finds its beat.

Across the fields where shadows lay,
New shoots rise strong, defying the past.
In the whispers of grass, we find our way,
In each sigh of wind, love everlasts.

So pause and breathe, feel the earth's call,
In soulful murmurs, our spirits entwine.
From scorched lands, we rise, never to fall,
A testament to life, forever divine.

Renewal of the Vibrant Spirit

In the hush of dawn's first light,
Awakening dreams take flight.
Hope dances on the breeze,
Whispers of joy among the trees.

Fields bathed in golden hue,
Nature's canvas, fresh and new.
With every drop of morning dew,
Life blooms, kissed by the view.

The heart beats strong and bright,
A symphony of pure delight.
Eager souls rise to play,
Embracing the warmth of day.

The rhythm of laughter, clear,
Echoes far, drawing near.
In the embrace of love's soft hand,
Fervent spirits take a stand.

As twilight whispers sweet goodbyes,
Stars emerge in velvet skies.
Time spins a gentle thread,
Renewed vigor shall be bred.

Resonance of the Phoenix's Heartbeat

From ashes rich, a new flame born,
In twilight's glow, the night is shorn.
Wings unfurl, in colors bright,
Soars the phoenix, takes to flight.

Echoes of fire stir the air,
In every heart, a silent prayer.
Through trials faced, the spirit grows,
In passionate hues, true beauty shows.

A dance of flames in moonlit skies,
Awakening dreams, where hope never dies.
With each beat, the world does hear,
The pulse of life, both bold and clear.

Transcending sorrow, embracing grace,
The cycle turns, a vibrant chase.
From shadows deep to heights above,
Resonates the heart of love.

With every dawn, rebirth is true,
A tale retold, anew and new.
In the warmth of the sun's ascent,
The phoenix sings, forever bent.

Lamentations of Tinted Leaves

Crisp whispers fall from branches bare,
Colors bleed in autumn's glare.
Every leaf a story told,
In shades of crimson, rust, and gold.

Gentle sighs of nature's woe,
As daylight fades, the shadows grow.
The winds carry a soft refrain,
Echoes of joy and hints of pain.

Beneath the boughs where memories cling,
The heart finds solace in the swing.
Each fluttering leaf, a fleeting thought,
In fleeting moments, truth is sought.

Nature weeps as seasons change,
Yet beauty lingers, never strange.
For in the loss, rebirth will start,
A circle drawn in nature's art.

As bare trees sway in hollowed air,
Life waits patiently, with love and care.
The bittersweet farewell does fade,
In every ending, hope is laid.

Odyssey through the Charred Wilderness

Through hallowed ground where shadows rest,
A journey stirs within each chest.
Amidst the ash and silent tears,
The spirit wanders, confronting fears.

Fires of change have ravaged broad,
But life endures through barren sod.
Amongst the scars of soot and smoke,
New shoots arise, a hardy cloak.

The earth remembers every cry,
In gentle whispers, spirits sigh.
With every step, the heart beats loud,
Resilience sings beneath the shroud.

Stars above, a distant guide,
Radiate love, igniting pride.
For through the dark, the light will gleam,
In charred remains, a vibrant dream.

This odyssey, both brave and true,
Bears witness to the past anew.
With every dawn comes healing light,
In the wilderness, souls take flight.

Whispers of Life Amidst the Charcoal

In shadows deep where embers glow,
A tale unfolds of life below.
Soft whispers weave through ashes grey,
As nature dreams, all else at bay.

Amidst the remnants, sprouts arise,
Their fragile forms reach for the skies.
In silence speaks the earth reborn,
A symphony of hope, each morn.

With gentle grace, the winds caress,
The charcoal past, no need to stress.
For life persists through darkest days,
In humble roots, the spirit stays.

The dance of time, a tender rite,
From ashes grow, a world alight.
With every bloom, the heart takes flight,
In whispers soft, the soul ignites.

Beneath the Scorched Veil

Beneath the heat where shadows wane,
A landscape lies, both lost and gained.
With every crack upon the earth,
Resilience whispers of rebirth.

The sun beats down, a fiery blaze,
Yet life persists in twisted ways.
From barren ground, green tendrils reach,
A lesson learned, the heart must teach.

In silent corners, hope may dwell,
Within each seed, a magic spell.
Through ashen paths, they claw and fight,
To reclaim warmth, to seek the light.

The fire may scorch, but hearts will learn,
To bend and bow, to twist and turn.
With every season, strength will rise,
Beneath the scorched, true beauty lies.

Murmurs of the Resurrected Grove

In twilight's hush, the grove awakes,
With whispers soft, the stillness breaks.
Each tree a story, roots entwined,
Murmurs of old, with hope defined.

Among the leaves, soft breezes sigh,
As shadows dance, the spirits fly.
They weave through branches, tales of yore,
In every rustle, memories soar.

From barren nights of silence deep,
Emerges life, no longer sleep.
In golden light, the tender shoots,
Reach for the sun with vibrant roots.

With every breeze, a promise made,
In verdant arms, the past will fade.
The grove resurrects, forever green,
Murmurs of life, in shades unseen.

Ghostly Chants of the Painted Skies

As dusk unfolds, the colors blend,
Ghostly whispers from skies descend.
Each hue a note in twilight's song,
Chants of the night where dreams belong.

The stars emerge, a distant choir,
A tapestry of light, desire.
In softest tones, the cosmos weeps,
In silent echoes, beauty sleeps.

Beneath the gaze of moonlit grace,
The spirits dance in endless space.
With every flare, the night ignites,
Chants of the universe, pure delights.

As shadows stretch, they weave and twine,
In ghostly chants, the worlds align.
No end to night, no start of day,
In painted skies, our dreams will stay.

Fires of Forgotten Whispers

In the night, shadows creep,
Voices echo, secrets keep.
Embers dance in silent air,
Flickering dreams, a whispered prayer.

Lost in thoughts of days gone by,
Memories drift, like smoke they fly.
Rustling leaves, a gentle sigh,
Nature's song, beneath the sky.

Fires fade, but stories stay,
In the heart, they light the way.
Whispers haunt the twilight glow,
Carried on winds, soft and slow.

From the ashes, moments rise,
Glimmering truths, beneath the skies.
To the forgotten, we must listen,
In the dark, our hopes still glisten.

Fires flicker, yet still burn bright,
Guiding souls through the endless night.
In the embers, warmth remains,
Life reborn through hidden pains.

Ashen Melodies of Renewal

In the stillness, ashes lie,
Softly whispering goodbye.
Songs of old, in shadows blend,
Melodies that time won't end.

Nature hums a quiet tune,
Beneath the watchful, waning moon.
In the silence, life anew,
Dancing sunbeams break the blue.

From the ruins, beauty springs,
Harbingers on fragile wings.
Each note plays its sacred part,
Resonating in the heart.

Awakening, the earth reborn,
Tender shoots from burnt-out scorn.
Softer winds, they brush the ground,
In their breath, new hope is found.

Ashen tales of yesterday,
Hold the light that leads the way.
Through the fire, we find our song,
In each note, we all belong.

Secrets of the Embered Hollow

Deep within the hollow's heart,
Where the flames once danced, then parted.
Whispers float on smoky breeze,
Telling tales among the trees.

Every ember keeps a secret,
In the dark, the shadows meet.
Woven tales of love and loss,
The flames once held, now bear the cost.

Ancient roots entwined in fate,
Guard the mysteries we await.
As twilight drums a soft reprise,
The night unveils hidden skies.

Lurking spirits in the night,
Guide the brave toward the light.
In their glow, the past revives,
Echoes dance, and memory thrives.

Through the hollow, whispers flow,
Carving paths where hearts will grow.
In each shadow, a light awaits,
Secrets told by the woodland gates.

A Symphony Among the Burnt Trunks

Amidst the charred and twisted wood,
Nature breathes, misunderstood.
Silenced towers, reaching high,
Crows converse with the crisp sky.

Each trunk tells a story lost,
Sung to life at timeless cost.
With every breeze, a note ascends,
In duet, the forest mends.

Faintest murmurs, rustling leaves,
Compose the symphony it weaves.
Harmonies of dusk and dawn,
In the stillness, lost and drawn.

Buried roots still crave the sun,
Sipping dew, their life begun.
Among the ashes, hope holds fast,
Resilient dreams from seasons past.

A chorus rising, soft and clear,
Echoing for those who hear.
In burnt remnants, beauty lies,
A symphony beneath the skies.

Enchanted Odes of the Resilient Trees

In the whisper of the breeze, they stand tall,
Guardians of ages, they heed nature's call.
Roots deep in the earth, they grasp the ground,
Their stories in rings, in silence profound.

Leaves dance in sunlight, bathed in gold,
They cradle the secrets, the wisdom of old.
Through storms and through trials, they bend but don't break,
Standing unwavering, for future's sake.

Each season they wear like a garment of grace,
From winter's cold grasp to spring's warm embrace.
With every new sprout, they share their cheer,
Nature's resilience, forever sincere.

Chants of Warmth Beneath the Frozen Night

Beneath the cold sky, where shadows creep,
A chorus of warmth stirs the night from sleep.
Fires flicker softly, embracing the dark,
As whispers of hope ignite a small spark.

The moonlight bathes all in a silvery hue,
While starlit secrets paint dreams anew.
Wrapped in the stillness, the world finds its peace,
In moments of quiet, worries release.

Beneath the frozen earth, life boldly waits,
For springs gentle touch to unlock the gates.
Chants of the ancients filled with desire,
To keep hearts alight, like a flickering fire.

Flickering Legends of the Blackened Glade

In shadows deep where whispers thrive,
Legends awaken, fighting to survive.
The blackened glade, where tales intertwine,
Each flickering tale, a glimmering sign.

Ghosts of the past in the twilight roam,
Carving their stories, calling this place home.
From ashes we rise, with courage we stand,
Breathing life into dreams once scorched by the hand.

The night saturates with echoes of lore,
Of battles won and hearts that restore.
In the dance of the flames, shadows take flight,
Flickering legends sung through the night.

The Soliloquy of the Renewed Blossom

From the warmth of the soil, a promise unfurls,
In colors so vivid, the heart gently swirls.
The renewed blossom breaks free from its sleep,
Speaking of courage in silence so deep.

With petals unfurling, it greets the sun,
Whispers of spring tell the tales of the run.
Each drop of dew cradles dreams of the day,
Awakening beauty in soft ballet.

Through storms and through droughts, it stands bold and bright,
An emblem of hope in the morning light.
A soliloquy sweet, nature's pure grace,
Forever reminding us of life's warm embrace.

An Oath of Smoke and Renewal

In the circle of ash, we stand tall,
Promises whispered by the old trees' call.
With each breath, the smoke we embrace,
Renewal begins in this sacred space.

Beneath the stars, the shadows play,
Burning embers guide the way.
In the warmth of the fire, spirits are found,
Binding our hearts to the earth's ground.

We cast our fears into the night,
As flames dance, igniting the light.
From hushed whispers to roaring cries,
An oath of smoke shall never die.

In the glowing coals, our stories merge,
History flows in a shimmering surge.
Together we rise from all that's dire,
A testament forged in sacred fire.

With each flicker, hope takes wing,
An anthem of freedom, we shall sing.
For in the ashes, our souls reborn,
We stand united, the promise sworn.

Night's Lament for the Wandering Flame

In the darkness the embers weep,
A flickering lullaby, secrets to keep.
For a wandering flame dances alone,
Under the stars, far from home.

Gentle sighs that ride on the breeze,
A soft murmur through the weary trees.
Night's lament flows like a river's dream,
As shadows weave through each flickering beam.

Promises whispered to void and sky,
While fragrant smoke drifts, eager to fly.
Lost in the stillness, we search in vain,
For the warmth of the hugs, the love of the flame.

Memories linger in the cool night air,
Where time stands still, and silence lays bare.
In the heart of the dark, a fire's refrain,
A steadfast hope in Wandering Flame.

Yet dawn will break with a gentle kiss,
Illuminating paths we cannot miss.
The night may mourn the flame that roams,
But tomorrow, the warmth will always come home.

Rituals of the Broken Branch

In the hush of the woods, a branch lies still,
Fractured and old, it speaks of will.
Leaves whisper secrets, a history worn,
Through the cycles of life, forever reborn.

Under the moon's soft, silver glow,
We gather the pieces, we learn to sow.
Each broken limb tells stories of strife,
Rituals etched in the warmth of life.

With gentle hands, we bind the fate,
Mending the wounds that time can create.
In the embrace of night, we feel the change,
Turning fears into dreams, vast and strange.

A promise made with every crack,
To rise from the shadows and never look back.
In unison, we chant our fate,
The power of kinship, never too late.

The broken branch bends, but does not break,
In the heart of the forest, new paths we take.
Through rituals born from fracture and pain,
We dance with the dawn, again and again.

The Quietude of Fire's Canvas

Glimmers of orange and gentle red,
Fire paints silence where dreams have fled.
In steady strokes, the shadows gleam,
Crafting whispers from the edge of a dream.

With every flicker, a tale unfolds,
Of ancient days and secrets told.
In the quietude where embers sigh,
We find the courage to spread our wings high.

The canvas glows with stories bright,
A testament written in warmth and light.
From the hearth's embrace, our spirits soar,
As fire's quietude unveils the lore.

Emotions linger in the smoky haze,
Lost in the dance of the flames' warm praise.
Every heartbeat echoes, soft yet grand,
Guided by fire, together we stand.

In the stillness of night, the world slows down,
A moment's serenity under the crown.
With fire as muse, we create and share,
In the quietude of art, none could compare.

Beneath the Charred Canopy

Beneath the ash, the whispers hide,
In shadows deep, where secrets bide.
Once vibrant life, now mute and gray,
Yet hope still flutters, a ghostly sway.

Through cracks and crevices, green will creep,
In silent corners where memories sleep.
Each fragile petal, a testament true,
To the strength of the earth, as it starts anew.

Scorched trunks stand tall, defiant, bold,
Holding tales of fire, stories untold.
As dawn breaks soft on a scarred domain,
The heart of nature beats once again.

Above the charred, a sky so wide,
Lessons of time in clouds abide.
Underneath, the roots intertwine,
Binding the old with a future divine.

So here we dwell, beneath exposed skies,
Finding new life where the old one dies.
With every ember, a promise is spun,
In ashes of yesterdays, we rise as one.

Songs of Celestial Rebirth

In twilight's embrace, new stars are born,
A symphony woven, the night adorned.
With every flicker, a story unfolds,
Of ancient whispers and dreams of old.

Through cosmic dances, the galaxies sway,
Echoes of birth in the Milky Way.
Each note a heartbeat, each pulse a flare,
Resounding hope in the darkened air.

Amidst the chaos, we find our place,
In cosmic rhythms, we seek solace.
The canvas of night, a tapestry bright,
Painting our journeys in silver light.

Winds of the cosmos sing softly here,
Lifting our spirits, erasing fear.
In the vastness, our voices combine,
Together we rise, in harmony's line.

So let us gather, beneath the wide sky,
With hearts full of music, we'll never say die.
In songs of rebirth, our hopes take flight,
Boundless and free in the celestial night.

Embers of Forgotten Dreams

In the quiet dusk, embers glow bright,
Faint traces of dreams that once took flight.
Whispers of wishes, now fading fast,
Like shadows of moments that barely last.

Each spark a memory, each flicker a sigh,
Remnants of hopes that soared through the sky.
With soft resolute hearts, we tend to the fire,
Nurturing embers with dreams that inspire.

Through the night's lull, the warmth remains,
Filling the voids, dissolving the chains.
In embers of past, new visions ignite,
Casting away darkness, embracing the light.

Through the ashes, a vision will bloom,
From forgotten corners, dispelling the gloom.
And though they may fade, these dreams we hold tight,
In every dawn breaks, lies a chance to ignite.

So cherish the embers, let passions rise high,
From forgotten dreams, we learn how to fly.
In the glow of the night, we'll find our way true,
As embers of hope guide us anew.

Reflections in the Resilient Twilight

In twilight's embrace, the world holds its breath,
Mirrored in silence, life dances with death.
Through shadows and light, the edges blur,
Glimmers of strength in the night's soft murmur.

Reflections whisper of battles once fought,
In the tapestry woven of lessons taught.
Resilience shines in the fading day,
A beacon of courage that lights our way.

With every heartbeat, we find our grace,
In the twilight's glow, we learn to face.
The trials and tribulations that life bestows,
Are threads of a fabric, each one that grows.

Embraced by dusk, we rise from the fall,
In the silence, we hear nature's call.
A symphony echoes in the gathering night,
Of dreams entwined, ready to take flight.

So let us reflect, in this resilient hour,
Where shadows may linger, yet light will empower.
In the tapestry of twilight, our essence we find,
As reflections of strength, we honor mankind.

Harmony of Flames and Memory

In twilight's glow, the shadows play,
Whispers of time drift softly away.
Embers pulse with tales untold,
A dance of warmth in the night so bold.

The flicker kisses the silent air,
Threads of the past, we gently share.
Each spark ignites a story dear,
In harmony, we draw them near.

Through crackling lore, our hearts align,
Captured moments, electric and divine.
Inscribed in flames, our laughter shines,
In this embrace, love intertwines.

The night unfolds, a canvas bright,
With every glow, we bless the light.
Let memories simmer, passions ignite,
In the dance of flames, we find our sight.

Together we rise, our spirits free,
Woven in warmth, a symphony.
From ashes born, our dreams take flight,
In harmony of flames, pure delight.

Alchemy of the Renewed Soul

In shadows deep, the heart awakens,
Through trials faced, the spirit quickens.
Where once was pain, new light shall glow,
In alchemy's grace, we rise from low.

Fragments lost in tempest's roar,
Crafting strength, we find much more.
Each tear a drop of future's gold,
Transforming scars, our truth unfolds.

A cycle ends, a journey starts,
Renewed in essence, we mend our hearts.
With every breath, the old reclaimed,
In soulful dance, forever named.

Embrace the light, let shadows fade,
In the forge of dreams, our path is laid.
From dusk to dawn, we learn to see,
In alchemy's arms, we are truly free.

Ever evolving, our spirits gleam,
In the tapestry of the eternal dream.
Through fire's touch, we find our way,
A renewed soul, bright as day.

Tales Woven in the Fire's Embrace

In the hearth's glow, old stories rise,
Echoes of laughter, whispers, and sighs.
Each flame a thread in the tapestry spun,
A legacy cherished, never undone.

With every flicker, the past unfurls,
In the blaze of night, adventure swirls.
Mysterious dances in ember's light,
Tales of the brave, lost in the night.

The wood crackles, a song in the dark,
Memory's shadows play their spark.
With rapt attention, we lend our ear,
To the fire's muse, we draw near.

From heart to heart, stories ignite,
Bound by the warmth, we find our sight.
In every whisper, a spark of grace,
In the fire's embrace, we find our place.

Through the smoke, visions dance around,
In stories shared, our souls are found.
Together we weave, with love defined,
In the fire's embrace, our fates entwined.

Rustic Echoes of the Eternal Dance

In fields of gold, the wild wind sings,
Whispers of nature, the joy it brings.
Rustic echoes in every glance,
Life in rhythm, a timeless dance.

Under the stars, we twirl and sway,
In moments captured, night turns to day.
With laughter and love, we take our stand,
In the cosmic weave, hand in hand.

The earth breathes deep in every beat,
Embracing senses, a life so sweet.
With every step, in trust we find,
In rustic echoes, our hearts aligned.

Through valleys wide, our spirits roam,
Carved by journeys, we call it home.
In twilight glow, we spin and glance,
For life's a song in the eternal dance.

Each sunset whispers a story old,
In warmth of twilight, the night's a fold.
Together we rise, through every chance,
In rustic echoes, we dance our dance.

Ashen Songs in the Twilight Grove

In shadows deep, where whispers blend,
The ashen air begins to bend.
While twilight dances, soft and slow,
Lost secrets pulse in twilight's glow.

The rustling leaves, a mournful sigh,
They echo dreams of days gone by.
Each breath of wind, a ghostly tune,
As stars awake beneath the moon.

Murmurs like smoke drift through the trees,
Holding tight all the memories.
In this grove, where silence rings,
The heart remembers what love brings.

Cloaked in night, yet alive with grace,
The ashes whisper, time can't erase.
Through ancient roots and stars above,
A serenade of hope and love.

So linger here, in twilight's embrace,
Let ashen songs find their rightful place.
For in the dark, the dreams ignite,
And hold the soul through endless night.

Echoing Hearts of the Scarlet Flame

In passion's glow, the embers spark,
Hearts collide within the dark.
With every beat, a fervent call,
In scarlet flames, we rise, we fall.

The dance of shadows intertwines,
Flames flicker, revealing signs.
Each heartbeat sings a vibrant hymn,
As light and shadow softly swim.

Whispers weave through fiery air,
In every glance, a daring stare.
Our echoes pulse in rhythmic spree,
Hearts ablaze with wild decree.

Through fierce desire, we seem to fly,
Touching flames against the sky.
In the warmth of this bright display,
We find our truth in passion's way.

With every flame, a story told,
In scarlet hues, the brave and bold.
As hearts unite, we dance the night,
In echoing love, we find our light.

Flickering Memories in Smoldering Silence

In stillness reigns the quiet sigh,
Flickering thoughts like smoke drift high.
Each memory, a shimmered thread,
In smoldering silence, softly spread.

The ghosts of laughter linger near,
In shadows cast, their voices clear.
With time, the warmth begins to fade,
Yet in our hearts, the film is laid.

Silence hugs the edges tight,
But flickers dance in the dying light.
Each moment passes, yet holds its claim,
In this cocoon, we speak their name.

Through smoldering ashes, we reflect,
On moments past, with deep respect.
Though time may wear the brightest hue,
In silence, we hold memories true.

So gather close, as embers fade,
Flickering thoughts, love never swayed.
In smoldering silence, we find our peace,
And let the echoes of our hearts increase.

Resilient Harmonics of the Forest Floor

Beneath the boughs where shadows dance,
The forest hums a sacred chance.
Resilient roots hold steady ground,
Harmonies in nature found.

In gentle whispers, breezes play,
Together weaving night and day.
Each rustling leaf, a note of song,
In vibrant choir, we all belong.

The pulse of life through branches weaves,
In every petal, hope believes.
With strength embedded in the core,
Resilient echoes evermore.

Upon the floor where stories bloom,
Life cycles through the ancient loom.
With every step, our spirits soar,
Embracing all the earth's rapport.

So let us walk this woodland space,
In harmony, find our true place.
For in the silence, we shall hear,
The forest's song, profound and clear.

Shadows of the Rebirth Flame

In the dusk where embers glow,
Silent whispers start to flow.
From the ashes rise anew,
Shadows dance, a vibrant hue.

Flame ignites the hollow night,
Casting warmth in fading light.
Hope emerges from the dark,
Kindled dreams with vibrant spark.

Each flicker tells a tale untold,
Of courage forged from fires bold.
Through the smoke and through the blaze,
Life reborn in radiant ways.

With every blaze a chance to grow,
Casting light on paths we know.
Embers flicker, shadows play,
In the rebirth, find your way.

So let the flames of hope unite,
Guide us through the endless night.
For within each shadow cast,
Lies the strength to change the past.

The Resilient Song of Fire

In the heart of flickering flame,
A song begins, a wild claim.
Resilient notes in air do rise,
Like phoenix wings in bright blue skies.

Crackling sparks in rhythm beat,
Echoing tales of brave defeat.
Through the trials, passion's chime,
Weaving strength in fire's rhyme.

Restless flames that will not tire,
Dance to the tune of ancient fire.
Each crack and pop a story shared,
In this symphony, hearts are bared.

Harnessing the light within,
We sing of loss, we sing of kin.
Through every trial, oh we sing,
The resilient song the flames do bring.

So let the fire's melody soar,
Carrying dreams forevermore.
In every ember's glow we find,
The strength of spirit intertwined.

Echoing through the Charcoal Woods

In the woods where shadows fall,
A soft echo sings through the tall.
Charcoal whispers drift and sway,
Guiding lost souls on their way.

Branches weave a draped embrace,
Holding secrets in their space.
Every sound, a soft refrain,
Lost in echoes of the rain.

Footsteps crunch on broken ground,
In the quiet, voices found.
Nature's breath, a gentle guide,
In these woods, we shall abide.

Twilight's cloak wraps 'round the trees,
Carrying hopes upon the breeze.
Shadows linger, yet they lead,
To the light where hearts are freed.

So wander here where echoes blend,
Through the charcoal woods, transcend.
For in the silence, truth shall bloom,
And find the light that breaks the gloom.

Twilight's Smoldering Reflections

As twilight wraps the fading day,
Smoldering hues begin to play.
Reflections dance on the surface bright,
Illuminating shadows of the night.

Softly glows the sky ablaze,
In a haze of orange rays.
Ripples break on waters deep,
Carrying secrets that we keep.

Whispers linger in the dusk,
Promises wrapped in twilight's husk.
Every glow, a tale to tell,
Of magic spun in evening's spell.

Through the dark, we search for peace,
In every shade, a sweet release.
With smoldering warmth, emotions rise,
Twilight's truth beneath the skies.

So embrace the fading light,
Let reflections hold you tight.
Through twilight's magic, find your way,
In the beauty of the end of day.

The Breath of Nature's Revival

Whispers of spring break the silence,
Blooming buds dance in the sun,
Gentle winds caress the branches,
Life awakens, cycles begun.

Raindrops kiss the thirsty earth,
With every drop, hope is sown,
Nature's canvas, vibrant rebirth,
In harmony, life has grown.

Butterflies flutter, colors bright,
Children laugh in fields of green,
Bees hum softly, pure delight,
Every moment, serene and keen.

Mountains cradle the sky's embrace,
Rivers weave through valleys wide,
In each corner, beauty finds place,
Nature's heart, our common guide.

Underneath the vast blue dome,
Seeds of joy in hearts reside,
Together we shall find our home,
In the breath of nature's tide.

Voices of the Phoenix's Heart

In the ashes, whispers rise,
From the darkness, flames ignite,
A song of hope, in the skies,
The phoenix soars, a stunning sight.

With fiery wings, it breaks the night,
Embers dance in the waking glow,
Each note a promise, pure and bright,
Through the shadows, strength will flow.

Chasing storms with fervent grace,
A tale of courage, old yet new,
Beneath the earth, a sacred space,
Where dreams are made and born anew.

Divine rebirth, a timeless tale,
In every heart, its echoes sing,
When one must fall, another prevails,
The cycle turns, a wondrous thing.

Together we rise, souls entwined,
In unity, our voices soar,
With every heartbeat, we remind,
The phoenix lives forevermore.

Parables of Ember and Ash

In the fading light, stories tell,
Of embers glowing in the night,
Each flicker holds a secret spell,
A dance between shadow and light.

Burning whispers ride the breeze,
Tales of loss, of love, of pain,
Through smoke and memory, we seize,
Wisdom gleaned from fire's reign.

Ashes linger in muted grace,
Lessons learned in time's embrace,
In every rise, in every trace,
A journey etched in every face.

Gathered close 'round the warm fire,
Hearts entwined in the passion's glow,
In parables, we find desire,
Where ember's warmth begins to show.

Though the flames may flicker low,
Hope endures in every heart,
In the ashes, seeds of growth,
From ember's spark, new dreams shall start.

A Canvas of Light Over Charred Remnants

On the horizon, dawn appears,
Casting light on the charred ground,
From the darkness, hope rears,
A canvas new, spreads all around.

Crimson hues bleed into gold,
Where shadows once held sober might,
Stories of the brave retold,
As nature weaves her threads of light.

From the ruins, life will spring,
Tender shoots reach for the sun,
A symphony of life to sing,
In the face of all that's done.

Each brushstroke, a memory lost,
Yet in beauty, we find our way,
Through trial, we count the cost,
In every dawn, a brighter day.

So stand with me, against the dark,
Let our hearts forge the light's embrace,
In the aftermath, we'll leave our mark,
Creating joy in every space.

Whispers of the Charred Dawn

In the quiet of morning's breath,
A shadow lingers, a ghost of death.
Stillness hungers for light to weave,
As the charred remnants dare to believe.

Soft tendrils of smoke rise slow,
Dancing hints of what we used to know.
Each whisper carries a tale untold,
Of moments fleeting, memories bold.

Through the haze, a faint glow sparks,
A promise sorrowed, a light in the dark.
The sun creeps forth, with tender grace,
Embracing softly every scarred face.

Songs of the past, in echoes they play,
As shadows retreat with the break of day.
From ashes born, a dawn anew,
Whispers of hope in amber hue.

With each heartbeat, a fire ignites,
Resilience rises, banishing flights.
From the charred earth, life will bloom,
In the whispers of the dawn, find room.

Flames that Memory Holds

In embers' glow, time stands still,
Flickering faces with stories to fill.
Each flame dances, a spirited trace,
Of laughter and love in this sacred space.

Memories flicker, a warm embrace,
As shadows weave in a smoldering place.
The crackle whispers of all we've lost,
Yet echoes linger, outweighing the cost.

Through veils of smoke, the past appears,
A canvas painted with joys and fears.
Moments ignited, bound by the soul,
Flames that memory holds make us whole.

In the flickering light, find solace rare,
As heartbeats sync with the evening air.
Old tales resurrected, together we dream,
In the flames' warm glow, we silently scheme.

Life's fragile dance in the fire's embrace,
With every spark, we reclaim our place.
In flames living on, our past unfolds,
Through the warmth of the fire, memory holds.

Beneath Ashen Canopies

Underneath skies where shadows cloak,
Silent whispers of smoke evoke.
Beneath ashen canopies, dreams reside,
In hushed tones where lost hopes abide.

Leaves fall gently, embracing the ground,
Stories of fire where silence found.
A world reborn from grief's gentle hand,
In the arms of the earth, we understand.

Time ensnares us in memories deep,
While the heart murmurs secrets to keep.
From charred remains, life struggles free,
Beneath ashen canopies, we see.

The winds carry messages, soft and low,
Of resilience born in shadows' flow.
In every hushed rustle, there's a call,
A testament whispered, in unity we fall.

In this sacred grove, rebirth takes flight,
Guided by embers that flicker bright.
Beneath ashen canopies, hope persists,
In the dance of the ashes, life still exists.

Reverberations in Ember Hues

In the twilight's glow, where memories sway,
Reverberations call from the ashes' play.
Each ember pulses, a heartbeat true,
In hues of orange, a vision anew.

The past lingers softly, a breath on the air,
With every flicker, a glimpse of despair.
Yet within the shadows, resilience burns,
Through reverberations, the spirit returns.

In soft cascades, the nightingale sings,
Of journeys embarked and the hope that it brings.
The canvas of dusk, with a fire's embrace,
Revealing the paths that time cannot erase.

Whispers of triumph and echoes of pain,
In ember hues, we bloom once again.
From fiery depths, our stories emerge,
Reverberations flourish, our souls converge.

In the silence of night, as shadows expand,
Life finds a way to make its stand.
Through flames and embers, we dance and renew,
In the reverberations of ember hues.

Harmony in the Ashen Meadow

A whisper lost in silent sighs,
Where shadows dance, and stillness lies.
Among the remnants of what was,
Hope flickers soft, a gentle buzz.

The grasses bow, in muted grace,
Embracing time, a warm embrace.
Beneath the sky, the colors blend,
In ashen fields, the dreams transcend.

Each heartbeat sways with nature's song,
In fleeting moments, we belong.
Through tepid winds, a story told,
Of love and loss, both brave and bold.

Together here, we find our peace,
In tender glades, the pain must cease.
With every step, the spirit grows,
In harmony, the meadow glows.

As twilight falls, the stars align,
In endless night, our hearts entwine.
A symphony of ash and light,
In perfect balance, day to night.

Stories Carved in Scorched Earth

In barren lands where shadows creep,
The whispers of the past run deep.
Each crack and crevice tells a tale,
Of hope and dreams that once set sail.

With every step upon this dust,
A legacy held in quiet trust.
The roots reach down, to grasp the fire,
Reviving spirits, dreams aspire.

A tapestry of pain and pride,
In twilight's glow, our hearts collide.
For all that's lost, there's much to learn,
In scorched earth's glow, our passions burn.

With hands outstretched, we write the lines,
Of fleeting moments, bright designs.
In fleeting embers, futures rise,
The stories live beneath the skies.

From ashes, strength and fire rebirth,
In every scar, there's endless worth.
Together, tales in silence share,
In scorched earth's heart, we breathe the air.

The Lament of the Eternal Flame

In flickering light, the shadows waltz,
Each flame's a tale, of love and faults.
It dances wildly, then grows tame,
A heartbeat soft, a whispered name.

Through night's embrace, it flickers bright,
A guiding star in the silent night.
Yet with each breath, a sorrow sighs,
The weight of years in embered eyes.

Yearning for warmth, but coldness flows,
In every flicker, the heart knows.
The flame that yearns to be set free,
In whispers soft, it calls to me.

Forever lost in time's cruel game,
Both light and shadow bear the same.
In every glow, a longing stays,
A silent grief in the glowing blaze.

The dance continues, a timeless quest,
In every flame, a soul expressed.
So let it burn, through night and day,
The eternal flame must find its way.

Flare of the Rising Hearth

In morning light, the hearth awakes,
With flickers bright, a warmth it makes.
Through gentle hands, the fire ignites,
Bringing forth love, and soft delights.

Each flicker tells of days gone by,
Of laughter shared, of whispered sighs.
Within its glow, the stories thrive,
In tender moments, we feel alive.

The crackling sound, a soothing song,
In every hearth, we all belong.
With every rise, the spirits soar,
In flames that dance, we find much more.

Together, gathered, hearts unite,
In warmth and love, the world feels right.
In every flare, a bond will form,
As we embrace the rising warm.

Through every season, fire will guide,
A beacon bright, where dreams reside.
So let us cherish this sacred space,
The flare of hearth, our warm embrace.

Ashen Whispers of New Beginnings

In the quiet shadows of dusk,
Hope flickers like a weary flame.
Each spark brings forth the dawn's rebirth,
Whispers of change intertwined in name.

From the ashes, new dreams ignite,
Softly kissed by the morning light.
Beneath the gray, the colors rise,
Awakening fortune in clear skies.

In the silence, the heartbeats sound,
Echoing tales of struggle profound.
The past may linger, but it will fade,
As new stories of courage are made.

With each breath, fresh promises bloom,
Casting away the remnants of gloom.
Through trials faced, we find our way,
In ashen whispers, we choose to stay.

The journey ahead is filled with grace,
Guided by light, we find our place.
In the tapestry of time, we weave,
Ashen whispers that help us believe.

Songs from the Embered Soul

From the depths of silence, a tune arises,
Melodies linger in the starry skies.
Each note a ember, glowing so bright,
Calling forth courage to dance in the night.

With every strum, a heartbeat's plea,
The soul awakens, longing to be free.
Songs of old, woven with dreams,
Resound in the heart, bursting at the seams.

In the fire's glow, joy takes flight,
Filling the world with warmth and light.
Echoes of laughter, soft and sincere,
Resounding through valleys, embracing all near.

As shadows dance upon the wall,
The embered soul surely calls,
To rise like smoke, in swirling flight,
Living in rhythms, lost to the night.

In harmony's grasp, we find our role,
Unified we stand, ever whole.
With songs that resonate through the dark,
We create legends, ignite that spark.

Legacy of the Ash-Woven Tree

Beneath the boughs of ancient lore,
Lies a tale of those who came before.
Roots anchored deep, reaching for grace,
In the heart of nature, we find our place.

With leaves like whispers that softly sway,
The ash-woven tree leads the way.
Branches stretch wide, embracing the sky,
Together with dreams, they soar and fly.

Seasons change, but the trunk stands strong,
Holding the memories, the stories belong.
In each ring, a year etched in time,
A legacy written in life's quiet rhyme.

From fallen leaves, new growth appears,
A cycle of life, through laughter and tears.
The tree stands watch, a sentinel proud,
Guarding secrets that speak loud.

Beneath its shade, we gather and dream,
Reviving our hopes, reigniting the theme.
For in every shadow cast on the ground,
The legacy remains, forever profound.

Flickers in the Twilight Air

As daylight fades, colors start to blend,
Whispers of twilight begin to send.
Flickers of stars in the dusky spread,
Painting the heavens with stories unsaid.

Shadows grow long, embracing the night,
Crickets begin their symphonic flight.
The world holds its breath, in hushed delight,
As dreams awaken in fading light.

In the dusk, a promise softly gleams,
Each flicker a dance, born from our dreams.
Moments collected, like fireflies caught,
In the twilight air, peace is sought.

With gentle sighs, the night draws near,
Guided by starlight, we conquer fear.
In the shimmering breaths of the cooling air,
Hope takes root in the darkness we share.

As dawn approaches, the cycle will start,
In every flicker, lies light in the heart.
Embrace the twilight, hold it so dear,
For within the shadows, love draws near.

www.ingramcontent.com/pod-product-compliance
Lightning Source LLC
Chambersburg PA
CBHW071546290125
21070CB00032B/954